LET'S VISIT CHILE

Let's visit
CHILE
GARRY LYLE

ACKNOWLEDGEMENTS

The Author and Publishers are grateful to the following organizations and individuals for permission to reproduce copyright photographs in this book:
The Anglo-Chilean Society; Art Directors Photo Library; Steve Benson Slide Bureau; Dr. Robert Gwynne; The Nitrate Corporation of Chile; Eugénie Peter; and Photothèque Vautier-de Nanxe.

CIP data
Lyle, Garry
  Let's visit Chile
  1. Chile – Social life and customs – Juvenile literature
  I. Title
  983'.064   F3060
  ISBN 0 222 00947 0

Burke Publishing Company Limited
Pegasus House, 116-120 Golden Lane, London EC1Y OTL, England.
Burke Publishing (Canada) Limited
Registered Office: 20 Queen Street West, Suite 3000, Box 30, Toronto, Canada M5H 1V5.
Burke Publishing Company Inc.
Registered Office: 333 State Street, PO Box 1740, Bridgeport, Connecticut 06601, U.S.A.
Filmset in Baskerville by Graphiti (Hull) Ltd., Hull, England.
Printed in Singapore by Tien Wah Press (Pte.) Ltd.

Contents

PERU
BOLIVIA
Arica
Iquique
Antofagasta
ANDES
Tropic of Capricorn
PACIFIC OCEAN
La Serena
Mt.Aconcagua
Valparaiso
SANTIAGO
Juan Fernandez Is.
ARGENTINA
Temuco
Chiloé Is
ANDES
Kilometres
0   160   320
0   100   200
Miles
N
Tierra del Fuego
Cape Horn Is.
CHILE
Chile
A.F.L.

Living on a Shoestring

When people from Chile say that they live on a shoestring, they are not talking about their household spending. They are talking about the shape of their country.

Like a shoestring, Chile is long and thin. Stretched out over more than half the west coast of South America, on a map it seems to have so little width that visitors are sometimes jokingly advised to wear waterproof boots—in case they have to step aside to let somebody pass, and find themselves with one foot in the sea.

However, there is no real danger of that. Chile is much less narrow than a glance at the map may suggest; it has that ''shoestring'' appearance only because of its very great length. In fact, parts of the northern and southern regions are over 350 kilometres (220 miles) wide, and the whole country has an average width of 190 kilometres (120 miles).

Chile is therefore about as wide as Portugal or the ''leg'' of Italy, but its 4,260-kilometre (2,650-mile) length gives it an area of nearly 757,000 square kilometres (293,000 square miles), and so makes it very much bigger than either Portugal or Italy—or than any of the other countries in western Europe.

Stretching as it does from the tropics in the north to a point in the south within about 800 kilometres (500 miles) of frozen

**Two of the contrasting physical features to be found in Chile—
the dry foothills of the Andes . . .**

Antarctica, Chile also has a wider variety of physical features, vegetation and climate than most other countries of the world. Each of the five natural regions into which its length divides is very different from the others; a visitor journeying through them feels that he is crossing a sample slice of the earth's entire surface.

The most northerly region, crossed near its centre by the Tropic of Capricorn, is a 1,000-kilometre (620-mile) stretch of hot and hilly desert, rainless and mainly lifeless, but rich in minerals. It has only one river and very few oases. The people who extract the minerals could not keep alive on what food may be found locally. Nearly everything they eat, as well as water and most of their other needs, must be brought to them over very long distances.

8

This region is called *El Grande Norte* in Spanish, which is Chile's national language. The name means the Big North, so it is not surprising to find that the neighbouring region—a much smaller one—is called *El Chico Norte,* the Little North.

At first, and especially in summer, there seems to be very little difference between the Little North and the Big North. However, visitors who take the Little North for another desert are much mistaken. Here, there is winter rain, sometimes as much as 500 millimetres (20 inches) over the season. There are also flowing rivers in the valleys which cross the region from east to west. And, with irrigation, the valley soil has been made very fertile. It grows tropical and sub-tropical fruits and vegetables, as well as fodder and grazing for some cattle and a large number of goats.

Here too is a reminder that although Spanish is Chile's national language, the country was inhabited before the first

. . . and the beach at Quintero on the Pacific

A vineyard in the Central Zone. The climate and soil make this area particularly suitable for agriculture

Europeans moved in. The original inhabitants were South American Indians, and the Little North still has several thousand of them living in much the same way as their ancestors did when they had the whole country to themselves.

With hot dry summers and semi-desert landscape made fertile by regular winter rain, the Little North is similar to some of the islands and drier coastlands of the Mediterranean Sea. South of it, is a region with a true Mediterranean climate. This is *La Zona Central,* the Central Zone.

Sometimes called ''the great garden of South America'', the Central Zone has up to 1,000 millimetres (about 40 inches) of rain in an average winter, and so has no water problems even in the driest of summers. Its very fertile soil produces great

10

quantities of grapes, oranges, melons, tomatoes, sunflowers (for oil) and every other crop that can be grown in almost perfect conditions of the Mediterranean type.

Here, in the centre of Chile, cattle-raising is another important rural industry. The animals are bred both for milk and for meat, and most of them have two changes of scenery each year. They graze on lowland pastures during the colder months, and are then driven up to mountain pastures for the summer. It is only during the summer months that these mountain

Threshing wheat in the Central Zone—Chile's most fertile area

pastures can be grazed, as they are usually under deep snow for the rest of the year.

This Central Zone also has most of Chile's factory industries, as well as its four biggest cities and nearly four-fifths of the twelve million Chilean people. Since the region is not much larger than the Little North and is very much smaller than the Big North, it may seem that such a large share of the population would have caused overcrowding. However, it is easy to forget that the country's "shoestring" shape is deceptive. The Central Zone is about the same size as England and Wales, which have more than four times as many people as the whole of Chile.

Among the many different farm crops of this region are chilli-peppers, a name usually shortened to chillies. These are the hot-tasting red pods which are dried and used whole in pickles and stews, or ground up to make Cayenne pepper. The name chilli came from one of the languages spoken by South American Indians, and some people believe that Chile is the same name spelt differently—but others disagree. Some argue that the country took its name from a word which means "peaceful" or "tranquil" in another Indian language; others think that it was chosen because it sounds like the call of one of the native birds; and these are not the only explanations. The truth is that nobody really knows. The first people who called the country Chile left no record of why they chose the name, and those who came later could only make guesses.

Chillies are also grown in parts of the fourth natural region, but not as one of the region's main products. They grow best

12

in very warm conditions, and the fourth natural region is very much cooler than the Central Zone—as might be expected of a region that is about as far from the tropics as the northern states of the United States of America or the south island of New Zealand.

The fourth natural region is also much wetter than the Central Zone. Here, the climate has changed from the Mediterranean type to what is sometimes called a temperate rain climate. This means that rain is likely to fall at any time of the year, not just in winter or in any other single season. Even the drier parts of the region have over 1,300 millimetres (50 inches) of rain each year, and the rest can expect up to about 2,500 millimetres (98 inches). With fertile soil, a temperate rain climate is particularly good for root crops such as potatoes and sugar beet, for apples and for pasture grasses.

The pastures of this region are very good indeed, and so it has become Chile's second cattle-raising area. However, these cattle do not spend the summer in the mountains. There is a mountain background here, as in the rest of Chile, but most of it is too steep, rough and bare for cattle. Such native wild animals as alpacas, deer and vicuñas might manage quite well on it, but cattle are kept to the safer, lower levels, where grasses thrive under an all-the-year-round rainfall.

Pine trees too are among the plants that grow well in a temperate rain climate. So are deciduous trees like the beech, of which there are large natural forests throughout the region. There are also large plantations of pine trees grown for making

The lake and volcano of Chungara, on the Chilean Altiplano

paper. Because of these many areas of forest, the region is usually called Forest Chile. Sometimes it is also called *Los Lagos* (the Lakes), although that name really belongs only to the southern part of Forest Chile. Here, the mountains look down on many lakes, some of them very large, and all of them beautiful.

The mountains are mainly part of the great Andes Range, which runs the whole length of South America, and rises to 6,964 metres (22,834 feet) in Mount Aconcagua, one of the world's highest peaks. Mount Aconcagua is just outside Chile (in neighbouring Argentina) but Chile itself contains at least the western sides of several mountains between 5,800 and 6,800 metres (19,000 and 22,500 feet) in height. The boundary between Chile and Argentina, and also between Chile and

14

Bolivia, runs along ridges of this range, whilst the dry brown Andes foothills to the north of Chile are crossed by the border between Chile and its third neighbour, Peru.

Near the Chilean side of this border is the northern end of another mountain range, much lower than the Andes. This is the Coast Range, which runs south above Chile's Pacific Ocean coastlands for about 2,500 kilometres (1,550 miles) to the southern edge of the Lakes district. Most of the farmlands, forests and towns of Chile are within the very long valley that lies between this range and the Andes.

Many thousands—perhaps millions—of years ago, the Coast Range continued to run parallel with the Andes right to the southern end of the continent. However, erosion and earth-quakes gradually wore gaps in the southern 1,600 kilometres (1,000 miles) of the range, allowing the sea to break through. In time, this flooded the whole southern section of the valley to a very great depth. Western foothills of the Andes Range became the new shoreline, and all that remained of the Coast Range section was its highest peaks and ridges, standing out of the water as a new archipelago.

This 1,600 kilometre (1,000-mile) stretch of western South America is Chile's fifth natural region. Much of it is solid, fairly mountainous mainland; but because it has so many islands it is called the Archipelagic Zone, or just the Archipelago.

The Archipelago's most northerly island is Chiloé, which deserves special mention because it grew the first potatoes ever brought into Europe. Chiloé is a large island, with an area of about 8,300 square kilometres (3,200 square miles), and a permanent population of about 150,000—mainly farmers and fishermen. South of it, hundreds of smaller and mainly uninhabited islands lie like a long strip of crazy stepping-stones over the 1,400 kilometres (900 miles) of sea to another large inhabited island, Tierra del Fuego—and then beyond Tierra del Fuego to the end of the Archipelago, Horn Island.

The most southerly point of Horn Island is also the "Land's End" of South America. It is Cape Horn, the high dark rocky headland famous for the violently stormy weather met by ships "rounding the Horn" as they pass between the Atlantic and

The Andes, Chile's natural boundary with the outside world

Pacific Oceans. These two oceans are linked by another southern sea-route, the long and winding strait between Tierra del Fuego and the mainland of South America. This strait was used, in the year 1520, by the first European to see Chile—the Portuguese navigator Ferdinand Magellan—and was given Magellan's name.

However, the Magellan Strait can be almost as stormy as the Cape Horn area. So, too, can most other parts of Chile's Archipelagic Zone. Island or mainland, this is not a place where the visitor can expect good weather. The whole vast region— nearly one third of Chile—is usually cold, windy, wet, or all three; and the sun can be seen on only about fifty days of the average year. Nevertheless, visitors who can stand up to the weather find much to see and enjoy—vast forests; fiords equal to any on the coast of Norway; volcanoes, waterfalls and hot springs; colonies of penguins and sea-lions; huge birds such as the condor vulture; glaciers which sometimes crack and ''calve'' icebergs into the blue-green lakes below them.

It is not only visitors who find the climate of this fifth natural region difficult. Chileans, too, prefer something milder, drier and sunnier, and so the entire central section of the region is almost uninhabited. The 350,000 people who do live in the Archipelagic Zone are settled mainly on Chiloé Island and the mainland opposite, and in the far south—on both sides of the Magellan Strait.

These areas have attracted people partly because the climatic conditions are less severe than they are in the rest of the

Archipelagic Zone, and partly because both areas have workable deposits of important minerals—including oil in the south. The oil-wells are mainly on the island of Tierra del Fuego, which is shared between Chile and Argentina. This area is also the main centre of Chile's prosperous sheep-raising industry, while cattle are bred in the milder mainland area opposite Chiloé Island.

Like their fellow-Chileans, the people who live in the fifth natural region are mainly descended from settlers who migrated

A Mapuche Indian woman near Temuco in Forest Chile

from Spain, or from Spanish settlers who married South American Indians. Chileans who have Indian blood are known by the Spanish name *mestizos,* which means ''mixed ones''. About four-fifths of the country's twelve million people are said to be *mestizos,* although the amount of Indian blood in many of them is now very small. It is also growing smaller, as very few full-blooded Indians have married outside their own communities in modern times. Members of these communities at present number about 150,000. Most live in Forest Chile, but there are some in all the other natural regions.

Especially during the last two centuries, Chile has also had immigrant settlers from European countries other than Spain— mainly the British Isles, France, Italy, Yugoslavia and Germany. These immigrants did not come in any great numbers, but they did make a major contribution towards getting their new country firmly and independently established, and towards hastening its development and progress.

None Better in the World

As far as we know, the first Europeans to reach South American waters were the great navigator Christopher Columbus and his rather mutinous crew. Columbus was an Italian, but he was working for the King of Spain and commanding Spanish ships, so it seems natural enough that Spaniards were the first people to consider using the new lands that Columbus reported.

However, they did not begin with South America. They went first through the Caribbean Sea to the eastern side of Central America, and established small coastal settlements on the narrow neck of land now called the Isthmus of Panama. From these settlements they soon found a pass that took them through jungle-covered mountains right across the isthmus. In this way, they went into South America from the western, Pacific Ocean side—not the eastern, Atlantic side as might have been expected.

Like Christopher Columbus himself, the earliest Spaniards to settle on the isthmus were not quite sure where they were. Many believed that they had come to some part of India. So they called the native people *Los Indios,* "the Indians". And those who went into South America from the western side of the isthmus found a large and rich Indian kingdom spread over the continent's north-western highlands.

The people of this kingdom were ruled tyrannically by a royal clan—probably of different blood—called Incas. The king himself was called the Inca. Usually, there was only one king, but when the first Spanish expedition arrived in 1532 the kingdom had become divided between two rival Incas. Greedy for the great wealth which the Incas displayed, the Spaniards saw this rivalry as a chance to gain power for themselves. By adding their strength to one side—as well as by using some trickery—they managed to take control of the whole kingdom.

The Spanish invaders here and in other parts of South America became known as *conquistadores,* ''conquerors''. It took them just three years to turn the Inca highlands and the coastal deserts below into the Spanish colony of Peru, with the new town of Lima as its capital. They put Lima on a lowland site, close to the coast. From there, in 1536, an expedition set out southward, to explore what is now Chile.

The Incas had already subdued the more primitive Indians in the natural regions which were later called the Big North and the Little North. So the Spanish expedition was allowed to pass nearly half way down the ''shoestring'' fairly peacefully—but not without great hardships in the desert, and great disappointment at finding none of the gold and silver which they had expected. After a year away, the survivors went back to Peru with nothing but bad reports of the land to the south.

The men of the next expedition, which left Lima in 1541, were more interested in finding land for settlement than in discovering precious metals. They took more kindly to Chile—

An equestrian statue of
Pedro de Valdivia, who
founded the first Spanish
settlements in Chile

especially when they had reached the fair and fertile Central
Zone. Indeed, their leader sent the King of Spain a letter saying
that the land was ''such that there is none better in the world
to live in''.

The leader who wrote so enthusiastically was Pedro de
Valdivia, after whom the city of Valdivia in Forest Chile is
named. Valdivia himself founded this city, and also two cities
in the Central Zone—Santiago (St. James), which is now Chile's
capital, and Concepción on the River Bio Bio, which flows into
the Pacific Ocean just north of Forest Chile.

Apart from a short time spent back in Peru, Pedro de Valdivia spent thirteen years in Chile. During that time, settlers and settlement spread through the whole of the Central Zone, but the Europeans could not get very far into Forest Chile. They were blocked by a large tribe of brave, warlike and very hostile Indians who called themselves the Mapuches, but were also known as Araucanians.

Before the Spaniards came to South America, the Incas had tried very hard to conquer the Mapuches, but the Mapuches had always forced them back. Now they were just as determined to keep the Spaniards out of Forest Chile. After years of raids and skirmishes, advances and retreats, their whole fighting force faced Valdivia's men in battle at a place called Tucapel. The Mapuches beat the Spaniards and went on to over-run half of the Central Zone before another Spanish force turned them back. They might have pushed even further had the Spaniards not killed their war-leader Lautaro. (He had once worked for Valdivia and had learned something about Spanish fighting methods.)

During the battle at Tucapel, Valdivia was taken prisoner. He was later killed very cruelly. As punishment for this, the Spanish governor who took Valdivia's place ordered the death of Caupolicán, the Mapuche tribal chief. That did not prevent the Mapuches from fighting on. They kept up their attacks on the settlers until finally the Spaniards offered to stay north of Forest Chile if the Mapuches would keep within their own lands.

The Mapuches agreed, but the agreement was often

broken—usually with bloodshed—and so it went on for nearly three hundred years. Only in the nineteenth century did it become possible for anyone other than a Mapuche to move freely and safely in Forest Chile.

However, there was plenty of room north of Forest Chile, and plenty of work both for the Europeans and for those Indians who chose to live at peace with them. Copper and other minerals were already being mined in the desert areas, and the fertile lands were being divided into huge *estancias* or *fundos*—farming estates raising cattle, or producing grain, fruit and wine in very large quantities with the help of very cheap Indian labour. At first—and for a very long time—a Chilean farm-worker was in much the same position as a serf in the old feudal systems of Europe. He had no wages, but worked for his food and shelter, and for the use of a small piece of land; and he broke the law if he moved away without his employer's permission.

The employers, too, were not as free as they wished to be, but the curb on their freedom did not come from feudal conditions. It came from Spanish trade regulations—regulations which treated Chile not as a separate Spanish colony, but as part of Peru. This meant that Chileans could not trade direct with Spain, their mother country, nor with any other country. All the goods they imported had to come to them through Peru. All the goods they exported had to be sent out through Peru. And that, of course, made imported goods much more expensive, and exported goods much less profitable.

This had two results. It encouraged Chileans to smuggle

goods in and out of the colony on British and French ships which kept well away from Peru. And it encouraged pirates, who knew that they could safely attack smugglers' ships, because the smugglers themselves were breaking Spanish laws.

Spain was very slow to legalize direct trade between Chile and other countries. And, when the regulations were changed, the Chileans were not very impressed. They had begun to think of breaking away from Spain, and becoming an independent nation. Spain might have agreed to independence had the Chileans agreed to remain subjects of the Spanish king. But that did not satisfy the Chileans. Under the leadership of a young soldier named José Carrera, they declared the country to be an independent republic, and stood ready for an invasion by Spanish troops.

The Spanish troops came, and Carrera's men were beaten in battle; but help was near. In neighbouring Argentina a similar rebellion was soon successful. Its leader José de San Martin was very cautious, believing that Argentina could not feel secure while Spain held Chile. He knew that the troops who had beaten Carrera were massed on the Chilean side of the Andes Range, ready to invade Argentina. So he led his troops on a remarkable forced march across the Andes, linked up with Carrera's defeated Chilean army, and took the massed Spanish troops completely by surprise. They were defeated and scattered early in 1817. Chile has been an independent republic since that year.

By then, Carrera's place as leader of the Chilean army had

been taken by a man with the Spanish christian name Bernardo but the rather un-Spanish surname O'Higgins. O'Higgins was the son of a Chilean mother and an Irish father who had taken service with the King of Spain, and had been sent to Peru as the king's representative. Bernardo had settled in Chile with his mother's people. Now, after his part in defeating the Spanish troops, he was chosen to be the first officially recognized president of the Chilean republic.

During President O'Higgins' first year in office, another man with an un-Spanish name arrived in Chile. He was Thomas Cochrane, the Earl of Dundonald in Scotland, an admiral in the British navy, and a hero of the wars against France in the time of Napoleon Bonaparte. Cochrane had found it hard to settle down in Britain when the wars were over. So he was delighted when Chile's new government asked him to take command of the Chilean navy, and build it up for an attack on Peru.

The Chileans—and also the Argentinians—thought it necessary to attack Peru because they believed that their republics would not be safe until Peru too became independent of Spain. They chose to attack by sea because Lima (Peru's capital city) lay close to the coast, and because an attack by land would have meant a long march over the Big North, which Chileans were by now calling the driest desert on earth.

Admiral Cochrane's ships were ready long before the Chilean and Argentinian troops who were to be carried in them. Meanwhile, the admiral sailed round the coasts of Chile and Peru,

26

A statue of José de San
Martin, the Argentinian
general who helped
the Chileans gain
independence from
Spain in 1817

capturing or damaging whatever Spanish ships he could find.
He also attacked and captured the Chilean seaport of Valdivia,
where most of the Spanish troops still in Chile were holding
out. Then, with eight warships and sixteen troopships—several
with British or North American officers—and with four thousand soldiers under the Argentinian General San Martin, he
sailed north to besiege Lima.

The siege was not a very long one. Lima finally surrendered
after a series of ''commando''-style attacks planned by Admiral
Cochrane and carried out by a fairly small number of General
San Martin's soldiers. Shortly afterwards, the Scottish admiral
and the Argentinian general were able to tell Chile's half-Irish
president that all danger of a Spanish invasion from Peru was

over. The Peruvians too had declared their country to be an independent republic.

But—like many other countries newly freed from colonial rule—Chile was to learn that independence can cause as many problems as it solves.

Fighting for Fertilizer

The 1,000-kilometre (620-mile) stretch of very dry desert in northern Chile is called the Atacama. Near the coast, the Atacama is just desert—not a green leaf, never a drop of rain. Further inland, it is mainly the same, but here and there regular heavy dew, or even a trickling spring, has moistened the earth enough to make plants grow, and form a small oasis.

When Spanish colonists began coming into Chile from Peru, they found Indians living in these oases, and some of the Spaniards—mainly Christian priests—chose to stay among the

A small oasis in the Atacama Desert in northern Chile

A typical scene in the Atacama Desert, which streches for 1,000 kilometres (620 miles)

Indians. Christianity appealed very strongly to the Indians, as it still does, and the priests became popular and important figures in the Indian communities. They were not only religious leaders, but also medical men, teachers, protectors against ill-treatment by colonists, and a source of knowledge about anything that the Indians found puzzling.

So it happened that one day some very frightened Indians came to their priest and told him a strange story. They had been out in the desert, and had piled up some large stones as a windbreak for a cooking-fire. But the fire was no sooner alight

30

than the stones themselves burst into flames, as did the earth around them. The priest was something of a scientist. So he persuaded one of the Indians to take him out to the camp site, and brought back the powdery remains of the burnt stones so that he could examine them. Then, when he had found nothing to explain the flames, he emptied the bag of powder on to his vegetable garden and forgot about it. A month or two later, he noticed that the plants where he had tipped the powder were very much bigger and healthier-looking than those in other parts of the garden.

The priest saw at once that the powder must have acted as a fertilizer. A check made by a chemist showed that it was a salt called sodium nitrate. Sodium nitrate usually catches alight if it is put near a naked flame. It is also one of the main foods needed by nearly every plant. And that was the beginning of chemical fertilizers which, in many countries, have now replaced such traditional organic fertilizers as cow-dung and decomposed plants.

The Atacama desert proved to have huge quantities of sodium nitrate, in the beds of a long string of dried-up lakes as much as 80 kilometres (50 miles) wide. So much of it was dug up and exported to fertilizer factories all round the world that it came to have a second name—Chile saltpetre, which means Chile rock-salt. Chile saltpetre has also been used as an ingredient of gunpowder and other explosive materials, although another saltpetre, potassium nitrate, is usually preferred for that.

Exporting sodium nitrate brought a great deal of money into

Sodium nitrate is extracted from an ore called caliche which forms a hard crust over much of the desert. This photograph shows caliche being broken up by blasting

Chile, but it brought trouble, too. The trouble was in the form of a very serious quarrel with Peru, and with Bolivia, another neighbouring republic which had also once been a Spanish colony. However, these were not the first of Chile's quarrels with those two neighbours, nor the first troubles to follow the winning of independence.

In fact, troubles had arisen almost as soon as Bernardo O'Higgins had become president, because many Chileans disapproved of him. One political party said that he was being too democratic; another party accused him of trying to be a dictator; several other parties complained that he should not have allowed the Argentinian General San Martin to have so

32

much control over the Chilean army. All this caused President O'Higgins to resign.

For the next seven years, many Chileans must have wished that they were still being ruled by Spain. Each party wanted its own candidate to succeed President O'Higgins. No party would accept the results of elections. The disagreements finally led to a small civil war. Then, in 1830, there was some agreement at last. A new president was chosen. But very soon it was found that he was not very expert at governing a country. Instead, he handed over the main work of government to one of his ministers, Diego Portales.

Unlike the president, Diego Portales was very good at governing the country. Though not a democratic man, he believed very firmly in fair treatment for everyone and in "the rule of law". He set a pattern of government which suited the majority of Chileans for many years.

Unhappily, there was still a small minority who preferred "gun law". These were supporters of Bolivia's aggressive and rather eccentric president Andres de Santa Cruz. Santa Cruz wanted to bring the whole of the old Inca kingdom together again under one head—himself. Portales saw this as a threat to Chile, and tried to stop it. As a result, some of Santa Cruz's Chilean supporters kidnapped Portales, and shot him.

The murder had the opposite effect to what they had wanted. Most Chileans were so angry about it that a war followed. It was a war with only one battle, which the Bolivians lost. Afterwards, Santa Cruz lost his presidency, the idea of a new Inca kingdom was forgotten, and Chile had forty peaceful years.

They were also years of great development and progress in industry, transport, overseas trade, education and social affairs. Chile had become a country that was making its mark in what was then the modern world.

These years were also the time when Chile received its greatest number of settlers from European countries other than Spain. Earlier, such immigrants had made the long journey across the Atlantic and around Cape Horn in ones and twos, but now they arrived in fairly large national groups. And sometimes they settled in national groups—as did German immigrants in various parts of Forest Chile, and Yugoslavs in the far south. Forest Chile was now open for settlement because the Mapuche Indians were at last allowing other people to live and work there.

Nevertheless, most of Chile's industries were still in the centre and the north, and now included work on the huge nitrate deposits in the Atacama Desert. Farmers in most countries had begun to use chemical fertilizers, and Chile was one of the very few countries which could supply the necessary sodium nitrate ingredient in great quantities. So Chile was earning an enormous amount of money from nitrate exports—enough money to make two of its neighbours envious. Bolivia and Peru now began to claim that a large part of Chile's desert area was really theirs, and they threatened to take it by force.

Once again, the Chileans chose to stand up to their northern neighbours; and once again their neighbours had the worst of it. In a war that continued for four years the Chilean army not only beat those of Bolivia and Peru. It also captured some of the nitrate-producing areas which belonged to Bolivia and Peru. These areas included the Peruvian seaport Arica and the Bolivian seaport Antofagasta, which was Bolivia's main outlet to the Pacific Ocean. Peace treaties allowed Chile to keep both the nitrate areas and the seaports. Since then, most of Bolivia's imports and exports by sea, and many of those of Peru, have had to pass through Chilean territory.

As a result of this war, Chile grew even more prosperous, and was soon considered the most developed and progressive of all the ex-Spanish territories in Latin America.

**Loading caliche
(nitrate ore)
after blasting**

Into the 1900s

As the twentieth century began, Chile might also have been thought of as a very fortunate country. It had nearly a monopoly of the world's most wanted fertilizer ingredient. It was working the world's largest copper mine as well as other rich mineral deposits. It had plenty of good land, and enough people to farm it but not to overcrowd it. And, because about four-fifths of the population—of all social classes—were *mestizos,* it had practically none of the racial problems that were troubling some other parts of the Americas.

However, Chile's good luck did not extend to politics and government. Even in the peaceful and progressive years between Chile's two wars against Bolivia and Peru there was serious disagreement among the four successive presidents and Congress, as the Chilean parliament was called. Then, as later, the main difficulty was that each president believed that he and his chosen ministers should have more power than Congress, while each congress was anxious to take power away from the president and his ministers.

On the whole, most Chileans usually supported their president rather than Congress, because the presidents were more likely to work for the benefit of the people. Although Congress was an elected body, at that time only a small number of people had the right to vote. These electors were usually the kind of people who preferred to vote for very wealthy land-owners, mine-owners and merchants. And, of course, they wanted the country to be governed for their own benefit, rather than to provide public services and social improvements only by taxing themselves.

In the years after the "fertilizer war", the disagreements became so serious that they drew Chile into another war—this time it was a civil war between supporters of the president and supporters of Congress.

The supporters of Congress won, and Congress then took away some of the presidential powers. Nevertheless, Congress continued to do very little for the people or the country.

Meanwhile, nitrate exports kept the country prosperous, and most of the people had work. Later, however, during the First World War scientists in other countries discovered new and cheaper ways of obtaining nitrates. As a result, Chile's nitrate industry lost its monopoly and many of its customers, and had to accept much lower prices from those customers who continued to buy. This caused a great deal of unemployment and other serious troubles which Congress could not cure. In 1925, Congress was forced to give up the powers which it had taken from the presidency.

The president then introduced new rules for governing the country. These became known as the 1925 Constitution. They set out exactly what both the president and Congress could do and could not do. They fixed the greatest number of years that

both president and Congress could serve between elections—
six for a president, four for both the upper and the lower house
of Congress. They also gave the right to vote at presidential
and Congress elections to every adult Chilean who could read
and write. They made voting at these elections compulsory.
They also ordered eighteen months' compulsory military train-
ing for all able-bodied men. And—among many other
changes—they took from the Roman Catholic Church the right
to consider itself Chile's official or state religion.

Most Chileans approved of all those changes, even the last.
Nearly nine-tenths of the population were—as they still are—

**The National Congress
building in Santiago**

Posters promoting the socialist party of Dr. Allende in the elections of 1973

Roman Catholics, but they thought it better that the Church should not have an official part in government, nor be in a position where it might seem to favour one political party rather than another.

The 1925 Constitution worked fairly well until 1970—allowing for the fact that during those years nearly every country suffered from the effects of the world depression of 1929-1931 and of the Second World War. One of those effects was the growth of political parties favouring socialist dictatorships of the kind now ruling the countries of eastern Europe. In 1970 a combination of such parties won a presidential election in Chile. The elected president was Dr. Salvador Allende (pronounced

Ah-*yen*-day). Less than one-third of the total number of votes went to Dr. Allende, but that was enough to make him president, as none of the many other parties or party combinations received even one-third (although one party came very close).

President Allende won his votes by persuading his electors that if the government owned and ran everything, everybody would be more prosperous. Things did not work out like that. The government was soon spending twice as much as the country earned. Production slowed down. Prices trebled. Shops ran out of goods and "black markets" began. Wages went unpaid. There were street fights, riots and strikes.

Then Congress accused President Allende of breaking a rule of the 1925 Constitution, and ordered him to resign. He refused. So Congress—as the 1925 Constitution allowed—ordered the army to remove him and his ministers.

Perhaps neither Congress nor the armed services expected the violence that followed. But violence there certainly was. During it, President Allende lost his life. Some say that he was killed in the fighting. Some say that he committed suicide. Many other people, on both sides, were killed or injured. Many of President Allende's followers fled to other countries. Many were arrested, and it has been claimed that some of these were treated over-harshly, and without respect for their democratic rights.

Meanwhile, the armed services had formed a *junta* (council) of officers to appoint a president and govern the country until it could settle down. The *junta* chose a military man, General Augusto Pinochet (pronounced Pin-osh-ay) as the new president, and dissolved Congress, postponing elections for an indefinite period, while things settled down again.

The settling down has taken a very long time. It will take even longer, but there has been a good deal of progress towards bringing back democratic government. This began in 1980, when the country's voters were asked to say ''yes'' or ''no'' to a new constitution. They said ''yes'' and the constitution is now in force, although the *junta* has retained the right to govern until 1988-89.

The main points of the new constitution are similar to those of the one adopted in 1925. It says that Chile is to be a democratic republic ruled by an elected president and Congress, the president to be elected for a term of six years, the upper

A view of Chile's capital city, Santiago, with the presidential palace in the foreground

house of Congress for a term of eight years, and the lower house for a term of four years. Both the president and the members of Congress are to be elected by all Chilean citizens, men and women, who have reached the age of eighteen. (People who were only ten years old when the new constitution was approved will vote at the first election, as it will not take place until 1988.)

However, local government under the new constitution has already begun. For this, the country has been divided into thirteen regions, each governed by a regional council, and the regions themselves have been divided into provinces, each with its own appointed governor. The most southerly region, Magellanes, is also the largest. With an area of 132,000 square kilometres (51,000 square miles) it is larger than some of Europe's independent countries, but it has less than one person for each square kilometre (only one person for every two square miles). These regions are political divisions, which also divide and sometimes overlap the natural regions at which we have already glanced.

It is only in matters of returning to democratic government that Chile has been taking a long time to settle down. Daily life and work have long been back to what they were before 1970, and in some ways conditions are much better than they were then.

For example, a scheme to build 900,000 houses throughout the country is well under way. These houses are for people whose present housing is far below standard—sometimes only a shanty, or a room in a house that was already overcrowded
42

Squatter settlements in Valparaiso

without them. The house will not be rented. Instead, when a family moves into a house built under this scheme they can think of it as their own, because the government will be helping them to buy it. The government, so it has said, aims to make Chile ''a country of property-owners''.

Chile is also re-planning its state education system. In the past, all state education has been planned and controlled by government offices in Santiago, the capital. But under the changed system each local area will manage and be respon-sible for its own schools. One aim of this change is to make education more suitable to local needs and conditions. The other is to see that more money is spent on building and equipping schools and on paying teachers, and less on the expenses of

43

running the system. When education throughout the whole country was managed from Santiago, expenses seem to have been extremely high, and often unnecessary.

In Chile now there are about eleven thousand schools, and the government runs about eight thousand of these. The others are run by churches and other private bodies, but many of them are helped by government grants. They include a number of schools which were originally intended for British and other English-speaking boys and girls but also have a large enrolment of Chileans.

No one has to pay for education in the government schools. In fact, Chile was the first American country outside the U.S.A. and Canada to provide free education for all children, although at first, education in Chile was not compulsory. As a result, for many years, Chile had a fairly large number of citizens who could not read or write. However, education became compulsory for all children up to the age of fourteen as far back as 1920, so Chileans unable to read or write are now fairly rare.

Because of Chile's ''shoestring'' shape, and because most of the people are concentrated in the middle of the country, children in the more remote parts often live a long way from the nearest school—sometimes such a long way, or on such difficult roads, that they cannot get to school even by bus. For these, the government has now begun to provide what it calls Rural Boarding Schools. At a Rural Boarding School, children go to school as usual on Monday morning, but they do not go home again on Monday afternoon. Instead, they live at the

44

school until Friday afternoon, when they go home for the weekend.

At present, there are nearly three million children at school in Chile, and many of them will go on to one of the country's eight universities, where their education will continue to be free. In recent years, the number of Chilean schoolchildren applying for university has been ten times as high as it was in the 1950s, but there is still no university in southern Chile, and only one in the north. The other seven are all in the central provinces, which shows what a population ''bulge'' there is in that part of the country.

Unlike many other modern governments, the government

The University of Chile in Santiago, which was founded in 1738 and now has over 55,000 students

of Chile does not like the idea of what is usually called the ''welfare state''. It believes that life is better for everybody if people earn enough money to pay for whatever services they may need or choose to have, instead of receiving them as ''handouts'' from the state. However—as with the housing scheme—the government is ready to help people if their earnings are genuinely too small to give them their basic needs. And, for all people whose earnings are still not as high as they should be, the state also provides health services, pensions and other welfare benefits.

Chile at Work

Before Dr. Allende became president of Chile, an Englishwoman on an expedition across the Andes lost her way in bad weather. It was a wild and empty-looking area, but she was lucky enough to find a *mestizo* shepherd family who gave her shelter and food.

The food appeared to be a kind of soup, greyish in colour, thick, and very hot. While waiting for it to cool, the Englishwoman asked its name. Her hostess answered with a word that sounded like "kwakka". Then she produced a container with a label that the Englishwoman recognized at once. It showed that "kwakka" was her hostess' way of pronouncing the brand name of the soup's main ingredient—Quaker porridge oats from Britain.

That story reminds us of two important facts about Chile. The first is that for many years most of the goods that Chile needed—including a large part of its foodstuffs—had to be imported. The second fact is that many of the imported goods came from Britain, or from other countries on British ships.

When Chile became an independent republic, much of the country was still undeveloped, and in much of the rest development had hardly begun. At the same time, Britain was leading the world into what is now called the Industrial Revolution.

British manufacturers were soon seeking overseas markets for a huge variety of goods made in factories using newly-invented machinery and engines. British engineering, mining and construction firms were looking for new areas which they could develop by using new skills and new equipment.

The Chileans had a long history of dealing with the British, because of the smuggling trade which had flourished during the centuries when Chile was ruled as a Spanish colony. So it seems reasonable enough that during the nineteenth century every second article displayed in many Chilean shops was made in Britain; that the man who was given the name *El Rey del Salitre* (the Nitrate King) because he came to control most of the nitrate industry was an Englishman named John North; that British people and firms had a hand in developing Chile's great copper- and coal-mining industries, in laying its railways, putting up its telegraph lines, planning its sea transport, building its roads and beginning its gas and electricity services.

However, it does not seem so reasonable that a country with such large areas of fertile land should have needed to import ordinary foodstuffs from Britain and—in much larger quantities—from other countries. Even as late as the 1950s only about one-third of the food eaten by Chileans was produced in Chile. The reason for this surprising shortage was that most Chilean farmers were not keeping up with the times. The huge farming estates, called *fundos,* produced enough for the hundreds—sometimes thousands—of people who lived on them. But they had little to spare for the growing number of people

Bullock carts such as this one are still used in Chile today, even though great advances have been made in agricultural methods

who lived in towns and worked in town industries or in mining. *Fundo* farmers had hardly changed their ways of working in three centuries. They were not interested in using the modern methods and equipment that would have helped them to produce more. As for other farms, their produce made no great difference. They were mainly very small, and the vastly spreading *fundos* had squeezed them out to less fertile land on the hilly fringes.

Nowadays, Chilean farming has changed a great deal, and it is still changing. After the 1950s, successive governments

49

began to break up the *fundos,* so that much of the most fertile land could become small farms run by independent owners who would use modern methods to make them more productive. Production rose steadily at first. But then, in the 1970s President Allende's government tried unsuccessfully to take over all farms and run them as state collectives, as had been done in the Soviet Union. On the whole, Chilean farmers did not like this. Nor did Chilean townsfolk, who found themselves paying more and more for less and less. They were all pleased when the *junta* under President Pinochet returned to a policy of private ownership.

The *junta* government also went back to breaking up *fundos* to provide more small farms for private owners. Many of these are now run co-operatively. Each farmer works his own land, but may make use of equipment held in common by all the members of his co-operative; and the co-operative has a marketing service which collects produce from all its members and then sells it in bulk. In this way, each farmer usually gets a better return than he would by selling his produce individually.

The result of all that—and also of land improvement by irrigation—is that instead of importing two-thirds of its foodstuffs, Chile now imports less than one-third. Whether or not it will have to import even less in the future is uncertain. It could, but at present it seems that the country can make more money by continuing to import some of its wheat and other grain, so that farmers can devote more of their time and land to growing fruit and vegetables for export.

Other crops which Chilean farmers grow in large quantities are potatoes, sugar-beet, tobacco, peas, beans, lentils, onions, chilli-peppers, sunflowers, olives, cotton and the clover-like cattle-food called alfalfa. They also keep about four million cattle, seven million sheep and goats, one million pigs and half a million horses. Horse-breeding is an important industry in Chile. And, of course, where there are cattle and horses there are cowboys. The Chilean cowboy is called a *huaso*. With a striped woollen poncho, tapering trousers and a flat-crowned hat, he looks rather different from the cowboys of North

Horses on a Chilean stock farm—horse-breeding is now an important industry in Chile

Huasos, or Chilean cowboys, in their traditional dress of striped woollen poncho, tapering trousers and flat-crowned hat

America, but his work is the same as theirs. So are his amusements—as visitors find when they see spectators queueing for one of Chile's many rodeos.

The pasturelands where cattle graze and *huasos* ride merge with the great forests, which are said to be the largest stands of timber trees in South America. Since the famous Amazon jungles of Brazil are also in South America, that may seem a rather doubtful claim. In fact, Brazil is Chile's second largest customer for timber and timber products. About forty other countries also import timber and timber products from Chile; timber companies say that production could be doubled in a year or two. The main timber products exported are hardboard, cardboard, paper, paper pulp and cellulose. Cellulose is used

52

mainly in making paints, varnishes, rayon cloth and plastics of several kinds.

Fisheries, too, keep a fairly large number of Chileans in work. Much of their catch is exported, mainly in the form of canned fish and fishmeal, and these exports bring in nearly twice as much money as the forestry exports. The Chilean coastal waters are particularly rich in fish, and Chile now ranks fifth among the world's fishing countries. It is even being forecast that fishing and forestry together may, in the next century, do what sodium nitrate did for Chile in the nineteenth century.

At present, however, the country's most profitable products are still minerals. There are about 70,000 paid workers in the mining industry, but in cash value they produce far more than the paid workers in farming, forestry and fishing, who together number nearly 700,000.

The main mineral product is now copper. Chile not only has the largest copper-mine in the world. It is also one of the world's three largest producers. Sodium nitrate, too, is still taken out of the northern desert in large quantities.

Though Chilean nitrate is not much used in modern fertilizers, it can be treated to produce iodine and one or two other very useful chemicals. Chile is now the world's largest supplier of these.

Chile's second mineral product is now iron, much of which is exported to Japan. Coal, too, is mined extensively. This comes from the largest coal reserves in South America, from which Chile now mines about 1,000,000 tonnes (984,200 tons)

Fishing is now one of Chile's most important industries. Because most of the fish are caught in coastal waters, many of the fishing-boats are small, like the ones shown in this picture

a year. At that rate, it can continue taking out the same amount annually for at least two thousand years.

Other minerals, including gold, silver, mercury, sulphur, borax and possibly uranium are also present in workable amounts. And about half of the country's oil needs are met from its own wells.

These wells, both on land and offshore, are in the far south, where the cold and windy climate is too severe for any other large-scale work except mining and sheep-farming. The main coal deposits are in Central Chile, and small amounts of copper,

54

silver and gold are also mined there, but the rest of the country's mining takes place mainly in the desert north, where the climate is too severely dry for most other work.

Between the arid north and icy south lie not only the great farming and forestry areas, but also the main factory towns. Chile's most impressive manufacturing plant is the steel works at Huachipato, near the city of Concepción. Concepción is on the southern edge of the Central Zone, a very long way from the iron-mines in the north. However, it is close to a coal-mining area, and as coal too is needed for steel-making it is easier to bring the iron to the coal than the coal to the iron. The iron ore comes by sea to Concepción Bay, which has very good harbours through which other goods are also imported and exported.

The open-cast copper mine at Chuquicamata in northern Chile. It is the largest copper mine in the world

Most of Chile's many harbours are much used by coastal shipping, for both cargo and passengers. Until the development of air services, sea travel was the only way of making any but the shortest journeys in southern Chile, and many people still prefer it. In the northern two-thirds of the country there are good roads and efficient railways as well as air services, but here too, goods and passengers are often carried by sea.

A feature of the 80,000 kilometres (50,000 miles) of roads in Chile is the independent truck-driver—a self-employed man who has his own truck, and contracts with mining companies, manufacturers and farmers to transport their products. There are great numbers of these trucks, particularly on the 3,000-kilometre (1875-mile) Pan-American Highway, which runs north and south along two-thirds of the ''shoestring''. Their drivers play a very important part in the working life of Chile and, during the time of the Allende government, they became a political force which influenced the future of the country.

All the main towns in central Chile are on or near the Pan-American Highway, and these towns make up Chile's main manufacturing zone. Outside this zone, most towns are mainly farming, mining or tourist centres. Within the zone, by far the greater part of factory industry is concentrated in or near the capital city Santiago. Santiago itself has about half Chile's factories; a good many of the other half are in the seaport city of Valparaiso, 130 kilometres (80 miles) to the north-west.

Some of these factories make goods for export—mainly paper and paper pulp, board, cellulose and various metal products—

56

but most are chiefly concerned with meeting Chile's own needs. They produce cloth and clothing of all kinds, processed foodstuffs, building materials, household equipment, cars and car accessories, petrol refined from Chilean and imported oil, cosmetics and other chemicals, and most other goods wanted for normal everyday use.

Some also produce souvenirs and other goods attractive to tourists. Shut off by the Andes in the east and the vast Pacific Ocean in the west, in the past Chile seemed too remote to draw many visitors. However, air services have put it within easy reach, and a growing tourist industry now looks after half a million visitors each year. Many of these come across the Andes from Argentina (by road as well as by air) and spend most of their time at Viña del Mar, on the Pacific coast just north of Valparaiso. Viña del Mar is not only Chile's largest and most popular holiday place. With a population nearing 300,000, it is also the country's second largest city and another industrial centre. Fortunately for visitors, the city is well planned and managed, and the factories—even the large sugar refinery— are not as unpleasantly obvious as are many in Santiago.

The City that is Chile

The English name James and the Spanish name Iago do not seem very much alike, but both are forms of yet another name—the Hebrew name Jacob. According to the Bible, there were two men of that name among the twelve apostles chosen by Jesus, and there is a legend that one of them travelled to Spain and preached the Christian gospel there.

Later, the Spaniards chose this apostle as their patron saint, and began to build a great church in his honour at Compostela in northern Spain. By then, they had put his name into its Spanish form, Iago, and joined it to the Spanish word for saint, to make the one word: Santiago. So they called the new church Santiago de Compostela. And, because Spaniards take their patron saint very seriously, Santiago became a very popular name for new settlements when Spain began to spread colonies abroad. Outside Spain itself, there are now at least twelve important towns called Santiago. To distinguish Chile's capital city from the rest of these Santiagos and various others, Chileans have given it the full name Santiago de Chile.

Santiago de Chile is almost in the middle of the country— about halfway between the Pacific Ocean in the west and the topmost ridges of the Andes in the east; nearly halfway between Peru in the north and the southern shore of the South American

A view over Santiago, towards Santa Lucia

mainland. As if to mark Santiago's central position in the country, a small but steep and very noticeable hill stands right in the middle of the city. Named after another saint, Santa Lucia, the hill has been made into a very fine park, with steps and paths leading through masses of greenery and flowers to the top, where Pedro de Valdivia raised a Christian cross and the flag of Spain when he founded the city in 1541. At the top now are a statue of Valdivia, and two forts built long after his time, to defend the city during the fighting that made Chile independent of Spain. One of these forts is now a museum of folk arts and crafts; the other is an observatory. It is from here that a cannon (safely, without a ball) is fired daily at mid-day, as a time-check.

At a height of about 72 metres (236 feet) Santa Lucia looks down into the main shopping, business and government area. This includes some stations of a fairly new underground railway, and spreads between a river called the Mapocho and the city's main street, Avenida Bernardo O'Higgins (Bernard O'Higgins Avenue).

Perhaps because Avenida Bernardo O'Higgins is rather a lot to say, most Chileans call this street the *Alameda* (Promenade). Lined with statues and flower-beds, it is about 100 metres (110 yards) wide for much of its 3.5-kilometre (2-mile) length. When it narrows, near the foot of Santa Lucia Hill, it leads eastward to join another avenue with a partly Irish name. This is the Avenida Vicuña MacKenna, named after a Chilean of Irish blood who was Santiago's most famous and popular governor.

When Vicuña MacKenna became governor in around 1870, Santa Lucia Hill had been little more than a rocky rubbish dump for about three centuries. But MacKenna set the convicts from the Santiago jail to work on it. In two years—without machinery or wheeled transport—they turned the hill into the magnificent park that it still is.

Santa Lucia is only one of the many fine parks which are, perhaps, Santiago's most pleasing feature. Where MacKenna Avenue meets O'Higgins Avenue, a square with statues leads quickly to the south bank of the Mapocho river. From there, both to the right and the left, a series of parks follows the river for almost the full width of the large mid-city area. There are

60

also parks off the western end of O'Higgins Avenue, and on the other side of the river. Among these are the two largest— San Cristobal across the river and Parque O'Higgins in the west.

From the bridges which cross towards San Cristobal, it can be seen that the river in this part of the city is really a wide, man-made canal, about 40 metres (130 feet) across from bank to bank. The natural sides of the river here were very soft and unstable and, as the city grew, there was danger that the foundations of buildings might be weakened, or even washed away. So it was decided to give the Mapocho a new man-made channel of cut stone. Since then, the water has kept in its proper place, and the city's foundations have remained dry.

61

The city engineers also drained a short and shallow branch of the Mapocho that joined the river from a south-westerly direction, and filled in the dry channel. That gave them a wide, firm foundation for a new street, which became the Avenida Bernardo O'Higgins

As in other parts of Chile, nobody in Santiago is allowed to forget the name O'Higgins. West of the mid-city area, a visitor has hardly finished walking the length of O'Higgins Avenue when he finds himself approaching the enormous Parque O'Higgins. This is really a vast sports area, with fields, pitches and courts for nearly all the games that are now popular

Shoeshines at work on a busy avenue in the centre of Santiago

internationally—and that includes a course for horse-racing. Horse-racing and other horse-riding sports are all very popular in Chile. For many years, a Chilean horse named *Huaso* (Cowboy) held the world record for height in show-jumping.

O'Higgins Park also has what it calls *Fantislandia,* an area which might best be described as a combination of fun-fair and amusements of the Disneyland type; and for those who prefer to keep still while they are being entertained the park has an open-air theatre. At this, there are regular concerts, dance recitals and other stage performances. Open-air dance performances (free) are also given in some of the other city parks during the warmer months of the year. These are very much enjoyed and it is often impossible to find a seat at one. Both ballet and folk dances may be seen at these performances, the most popular folk dance being the *cueca,* a dance something like the Spanish *flamenco.*

Vast as it is, O'Higgins Park is smaller than San Cristobal across the river, since San Cristobal not only has length and breadth, but also height. Like Santa Lucia, San Cristobal is a hill, but a hill very much larger and taller than its sister on the north side of the Mapocho. It stands about 360 metres (1,200 feet) high, can be climbed in comfort by cable railway, and is famous for three features—views, a zoo and a statue. The views are not only across the skyscrapers, the less modern buildings, the smoky factories and the open spaces of the city. They stretch as far as the snowy central peaks of the Andes, about 100 kilometres (62 miles) away.

At the zoo, the inhabitants are international—although, naturally enough, the representative range of wildlife native to Chile is especially large. Whether Chilean or not, the animals have living conditions which could hardly be achieved in a zoo on fairly level ground. Because this zoo spreads over much of a varied hillside, it has been possible to put each type of animal into surroundings similar to those which it would have in the wild. The statue which stands on the hill's highest point came to Chile as a present from France. It is a huge figure of the Virgin Mary. A very impressive sight by day, the statue is even more impressive at night, when it is lit up so brightly that it may be seen from the other side of the city. Some people, however, have more affection for a much smaller statue of the Virgin Mary, kept in a church down on O'Higgins Avenue, between the National Library and Chile's main university. Only about 27 centimetres (11 inches) long, it came south on Pedro de Valdivia's first journey from Peru, fastened to the pommel of his saddle.

The church where Franciscan monks keep this small statue of Mary may be the oldest in Santiago. It is certainly one of the few city buildings which are nearly as old as the city itself. The other buildings which look old date only from the nineteenth century, and the rest of the city—from shanties to skyscrapers up to twenty-two stories high—obviously belongs to the twentieth century. The shanties are called *callampas* (mushrooms), because they seem to spring up overnight as more and more people crowd into Santiago to work in its expanding factory industries. However, they should appear less in future, as the government's house-building scheme progresses.

Among the older-looking buildings, the biggest, called *Palacio de la Moneda,* fills in a whole city block off the western section of O'Higgins Avenue. It was damaged during the fighting when President Allende was removed from office, but has now been fully restored. The Spanish name *Palacio de la Moneda* could be translated as Money Palace, but this building is not a mint. Nor has it anything directly to do with the coins called *pesos* and *centavos* which are the Chilean units of currency. With some words, the Spanish language spoken in Chile is different from the Spanish of Spain, and the word *moneda* is one of these. In Chile, if *moneda* is spelt with a capital M, its meaning changes from ''money'' to ''government'', so *Palacio de la Moneda* really means Government Palace. And this building, whose name is usually shortened to *La Moneda,* is the official residence of Chile's presidents. It also contains some of the government offices.

Most of the skyscrapers and other large buildings spread around *La Moneda* are also government offices. That helps to explain why the saying ''Santiago is Chile'' has been fairly common among Chileans. Until recently, Chile had very little local government. Nearly everything to do with government matters, however small, was decided, planned, arranged and managed in *La Moneda* and the government buildings around it. So people in the remoter regions felt that they were expected to make the best of what was good for the Santiago area— however unsuitable it was for them.

These Chileans should now have much less reason for feeling that they are usually "left out in the cold". The present government's policies for education and public health make it clear that in future local communities are to have much more responsibility for their own affairs, and will be much less dependent upon decisions made in the buildings around *La Moneda*.

However, that will not completely rid them of the "Santiago is Chile" feeling. Not only is Santiago almost in the middle of Chile. It is also nearly in the middle of the natural region which, to most Chileans, is the best for everyday living and everyday working. They find that it has the best climate, the most fertile soil, the most pleasing and varied scenery, and the greatest concentration of natural resources. And that is why

66

Chile's centre of government, its main town industries, its great commercial undertakings and its most important educational and cultural institutions have become firmly established there. It is also, of course, why nearly four-fifths of the Chilean people live in the region, and why about two-fifths of them live in Santiago itself or in the two large neighbouring cities of Valparaiso and Viña del Mar.

With so many people and so much activity concentrated into such a relatively small area, Santiago must surely continue being seen as "the city that is Chile".

For the capital city of a country which depends very much on imports and exports, the position of Santiago has one disadvantage. It is too far from the sea to be its own seaport. Instead, it has had to make use of Valparaiso, which has been Chile's

Valparaiso, Chile's main seaport

main seaport since long before 1818, when the government of President O'Higgins made Santiago the official capital of the republic. In fact, Valparaiso was being used as a seaport several years before Santiago was founded—although its present appearance hardly suggests that. Much of the city was destroyed by an earthquake in 1906, and there had been serious earthquakes in earlier centuries. So most of modern Valparaiso—from high-rise buildings on the waterfront to shanties cluttering hillsides 455 metres (1,500 feet) above—is fairly new.

The hillsides are part of the Coast Range, and the residential areas of the city spread up the slopes in a maze of terraces, steps and narrow winding lanes. Parts of these slopes cannot be reached by car, but cable railways connect all of them with the business and industrial areas down on the lower levels, although anyone who needs more transport at the upper ends of the railways may well have to use a mule.

However, people who live on those higher levels are compensated at the New Year. Then, they have a particularly good view of the main feature of Valparaiso's New Year festivities—a highly spectacular display of fireworks over the harbour. Watchers usually have a dry, warm evening for the display. As Chile is in the southern hemisphere, the New Year comes at midsummer.

For those who live on lower levels, a favourite place for looking at the fireworks—and at magnificent sea views by daylight—is a high promenade below the Naval College, which stands on a hilltop near the western end of the harbour. The promenade is reached not by a cable railway, but by a public outdoor lift which carries passengers straight up from a square near the waterfront.

Another popular viewing-point—and one with a very well-known name—is the Miradero O'Higgins (O'Higgins Lookout). This stands above the eastern end of the harbour, and is named after Bernardo O'Higgins because he used it to watch Admiral Cochrane's ships setting out to attack Peru in their attempt to remove the Spanish colonial government. As his eyes followed the ships, he is supposed to have said that the future of America depended upon them—and, if he did say that, he was right. Very few parts of the Americas, north or south, were not changed in one way or another when Spain was forced to give up its American colonies.

The name Valparaiso means Paradise Valley. Perhaps the place seemed like that to the early Spanish settlers, especially after a hot, hard march over the northern deserts, or a rough but risky voyage in a small sailing-ship. Today, they would have to think of another name. Modern Valparaiso is interesting, impressive, and even exciting to those who want excitement, but a paradise it certainly is not. Most visitors find it a cramped, noisy, untidy and in parts rather ramshackle and grubby industrial seaport, lucky enough to have beautiful surroundings and a very pleasant climate. If they used the word paradise at all, they would be more inclined to use it of Viña del Mar, which has spread so much in recent years that it seems almost like a better-looking half of Valparaiso.

Viña del Mar, a popular tourist resort also known as the ''Garden City''

Viña del Mar is a more down-to-earth name than Valparaiso. It means Vineyard by the Sea and, although the vineyard is now lost under the homes and workplaces of 300,000 people, the name still seems suitable because of the city's many gardens. In fact, Viña has often been called the Garden City.

Of all the public and private gardens which have given Viña that second name, the most striking are those of *Quinta Vergara*, which was once a private house but is now an art gallery and training-school for artists. The house itself is approached by a double avenue of palm trees. And the huge grounds contain an open-air theatre as well as the beautiful flower-gardens. Ballet and other entertainments are staged here during the warmer

70

months, and in the summer-holiday season it is used for a very popular five-day international song festival.

Quinta Vergara has Viña's most famous gardens, but the city's most famous house stands on a high headland overlooking a bridged lagoon. The headland is called Cerro Castillo (Castle Hill), and the house is the summer residence of Chile's presidents.

Below Cerro Castillo, on the other side of the lagoon and also surrounded by beautiful gardens, is the Viña Casino, internationally known not only for gambling, but also as an entertainment centre. Unlike gambling establishments in many other countries, the Viña Casino is run by the city council, and the very large profits are used for the upkeep and improvement of the city.

The old mansion, *Quinta Vergara,* now Viña del Mar's art gallery and art school

Between 1934 and 1964, the population of Valparaiso increased by about forty per cent. The figure then began to go down and, at 266,000, it is still lower than it was in 1964. Over the same years, Viña del Mar's population rose by nearly six hundred per cent, giving Viña more people than Valparaiso, and making it Chile's second city.

Social changes after the Second World War caused much of the increase. More and more people, both in Chile and in neighbouring countries, began to take an annual holiday away from home. Viña del Mar had long stretches of good beaches, an attractive forest background, sports facilities of many kinds, plenty of entertainment, and was easily reached from Santiago. So it naturally attracted holiday-makers, and the permanent population was increased by the large number of people who moved in to look after them. Social changes also increased the number of retired people able to afford a permanent move to holiday resorts; and, as so many Chileans live in and around Santiago, they naturally think of Viña as a place to retire to.

Viña's industrial areas are so carefully kept in the background that it is easy to forget industry's part in the city's fast development. Many of the increased population are not retired people, nor younger people who have no need to work, nor people looking after the needs of holiday visitors. They are industrial workers employed in a variety of factories which prove—as we have already seen—that a city can be a busy and productive industrial centre without this affecting its other features and activities, or disfiguring the environment.

North, Centre and South

If you go to the bus station in Santiago and ask to be put on the bus that makes the longest journey, you will get off in the city of Arica, twenty-seven hours and about 2,100 kilometres (1,300 miles) later. Arica is Chile's most northerly city. It stands among sand-dunes on the coastal edge of the Atacama Desert, less than 20 kilometres (13 miles) from the frontier between Chile and Peru.

The frontier was once well to the south of Arica, not to the north as it is now. It was moved to the north after the ''fertilizer war'' of 1879-1883, when Chile gained a long section of the Atacama Desert—including Arica—from Bolivia and Peru. That left Peru without a southern seaport, and Bolivia without a seaport at all. So Arica now lives mainly by handling about half of Bolivia's imports and exports, and some of Peru's.

In the past, most of the goods handled have travelled to and from Arica by rail; but recently the line into Bolivia has had competition from road transport on a new branch of the Pan-American Highway. Arica is also the ocean terminal of a pipeline from Bolivia, which has very productive oilfields in the foothills of the Andes.

These northern coastlands are a long line of bare, pinkish cliffs up to nearly 1,000 metres (3,300 feet) high. Coastal towns

Arica Headland. Chilean troops sealed this headland to fight and win a decisive battle in the ''fertilizer war''. A Chilean flag always flies above the battlefield

like Arica lie at their feet, in places where the sea has worn away sections of cliff-face to make patches of rocky, fairly level land.

The towns have no more rain than the very dry desert above, but most—like Arica—are within reach of oases. So the people are in no danger of going wholly without fresh food. However, there are other dangers. For example, the Atacama Desert, like everywhere else in sight of the Andes, is subject to earthquakes. Coastal earthquakes are sometimes followed by tidal waves. In 1905 such a tidal wave washed away a great deal of Arica, including all its churches. As it happened, the town of Ilo, just over the border in Peru, had a prefabricated church which had been made for it after a similar disaster. It was a large church, designed by no less a person than Gustave Eiffel (the French engineer who built the famous Eiffel Tower in Paris). And, like the Eiffel Tower, the Ilo church was made of iron. So it was

74

shipped to Arica like the pieces of a great toy model, and put together again in Arica's main square.

It became the city's main church, the cathedral of San Màrcos, and it is still there—a very popular tourist attraction. So too is another piece of ironwork, which stands outside the city's railway station. This is the last steam-powered engine used on the line between Arica and La Paz, the political capital of Bolivia.

Arica's tourists are mainly from Bolivia (a land-locked country). For them, Arica is the nearest place in which to have a seaside holiday. They would hardly be interested in a long excursion inland, especially as it would take them almost back home. But most other visitors like to spend at least a day in the Parque Nacional Lauca (Lauca National Park) on a bleak plateau called the Altiplano, 3,500 metres (11,500 feet) and

A herd of llamas on the Chilean Altiplano

more up in the Andes. The reasons for coming here are the views and wildlife—the views being mainly of volcanoes with snow on their slopes and of intensely blue lakes; the wildlife including flamingos and other waterfowl, condors, rheas, alpacas, vicuñas, llamas and even an occasional puma. (The rhea is a flightless bird sometimes called the South American ostrich.) Llamas and alpacas are also bred and used as farm and working animals in the drier and higher mountain regions. Here too their dung is often used as fuel for fires—since there is no local wood available on the arid plateau.

None of Chile's northern cities is very big. Arica has less than 120,000 people. The next city to the south, Iquique, has just over 100,000. Iquique is about 170 kilometres (105 miles) from Arica. The road to it passes through a town that is large, but seems to be almost dead, and has a name that usually surprises English-speaking visitors—the very English-sounding name Humberstone. It was named after John Humberstone, one of the many British people who played an important part in developing the nitrate industry. The town itself was once an important nitrate centre, but when its nitrate deposits became too expensive to work, there was nothing else to keep it alive.

The city of Iquique was more fortunate. It did find something else to keep it going when the nitrate industry began to decline. It began to expand and develop its fishing industry, and now exports great quantities of canned fish, fish oil and fishmeal. Fishmeal is a factory product used mainly for feeding cattle. Salt, too, is exported in large quantities from Iquique. Chile

The Opera House in Iquique, built in 1895 with money from the nitrate industry. The mountains on the left of the picture form part of the Coastal Range

claims to have enough salt to supply all that the world might want for several thousand years.

Iquique has also gone into shipbuilding. Using Chilean steel, a harbourside shipyard is making fishing craft and other small vessels. However, when Chileans hear of the harbour at Iquique they are more likely to think of ship-sinking than ship-building. It was here, at the start of the "fertilizer war" that two small Chilean ships fought an heroic battle against much stronger vessels from Peru. The city's bright and handsome main square, Plaza Arturo Prat, is named after the commander of the Chilean ships, who lost his life in the battle. Many streets, squares and other local features throughout the country are also named after him.

Iquique stands almost midway between Arica and northern Chile's largest city, Antofagasta. The Antofagasta area was once Bolivian territory but, like Arica, was captured by Chile during the "fertilizer war". However, Bolivia did not lose the use of its harbour. Antofagasta now handles all the Bolivian imports and exports that do not pass through Arica. The goods which pass through the port travel from and to Bolivia by a railway that was built—and is partly owned—by a British company. This railway does not carry passengers over the full length of the line, and Antofagasta's other international railway—over the Andes to Argentina—has recently stopped carrying passengers altogether.

Antofagasta is also the port for most of the Chilean nitrate deposits that are still being worked, and for the huge open-cast copper-mine at Chuquicamata, 3,000 metres (10,000 feet) up in the mountains. Chuquicamata was opened and developed by a United States mining company, but it is now owned and managed by Chileans.

Handling exports and imports is not the only way of making a living in Antofagasta. Many of the city's 160,000 people work in factories producing a variety of goods to meet the needs of towns and mining communities throughout the Atacama and the semi-desert zone further south. It also has working shipyards and—like most other towns on the north coast—is a centre for seaside holiday-makers and sea-anglers. Even on the hottest

78

days, Chile's northern shores are kept pleasantly cool by the waters of the Humboldt Current, which flows from the Antarctic area north towards the Equator.

In an area with practically no rainfall, Antofagasta is a man-made oasis with parks and squares that show a luxuriant growth of trees and garden flowers.

About 400 kilometres (250 miles) south of Antofagasta, the Atacama Desert ends where the River Copiapó flows across Chile from east to west. On this river a small city, also called Copiapó, is the main centre for a large mining area producing chiefly iron, copper, gold and silver, and for a fertile farming valley well watered by the river. The city lies inland, and in sight of the permanent snows on the active volcano named Ojos

The Anglo-Chilean clock tower in Antofagasta, donated by British residents

del Salado. About fifty of Chile's two thousand volcanoes are active, but at 6,890 metres (22,590 feet) Ojos del Salado is the highest. Some people believe that it is also the highest of all the peaks in the Andes, as a fairly recent measurement suggested that it is really 123 metres (403 feet) higher than Mount Aconcagua. However, that has not yet been fully checked.

During the boom mining years of the nineteenth century, Copiapó was much better-known and more important than it is now. In fact, when a famous French actress of the time visited Chile, she chose to perform in Copiapó rather than in Santiago. In our own time, it still has importance as a mining centre, but its population is well below 100,000, and it could hardly be said to rival the capital city.

Over the 850 kilometres (530 miles) between Copiapó and Santiago, the most interesting city is certainly La Serena—and not only because the great English seafarer Sir Francis Drake is supposed to have buried treasure near by when he sailed along the coast of Chile 400 years ago. To the visitor, La Serena is interesting mainly for its very Spanish appearance. Over all, there is not a great deal in the buildings of Chile to suggest that the country was once a Spanish colony, or that the people are mainly of Spanish descent. This did not please Don Gabriel Gonzalez Videla, a La Serena man who had been president of the republic. So he took an opportunity to re-plan and rebuild much of his native town in the Spanish style. The work was done very successfully, and La Serena is now a ''living museum'' of Spanish colonial architecture.

The La Serena district was also the birthplace of Chile's best-known woman. She was the poet Gabriela Mistral, who won the International Nobel Prize for Literature in 1945. She also held high posts in Chilean education and as a representative of the Chilean government abroad.

Unlike the cities further north, La Serena does not have much to do with mining. It also leaves factory industries to the neighbouring seaport city of Coquimbo, which is only about 10 kilometres (6 miles) away. Its own work is marketing farm produce and flowers, and looking after a large number of visitors. The visitors come not only to see the city itself, but also to use some very good beaches and to watch some of the best rodeos in the country. If they happen to be there on 18th September, they also find themselves caught up in an entertainment that they did not expect. The first declaration that Chile was to be an independent republic was made in La Serena, and each year on the anniversary there is an enormous public beach picnic.

Each year at Christmas (midsummer), visitors may also see the Christian religious festival of the Virgin of the Rosary, in a village called Andacolla, which lies within easy reach of La Serena. The Virgin is a statue which is believed to have made some miraculous cures. On the days of the festival, up to about 100,000 pilgrims dance continually in and around the church where the statue is kept, to the music of traditional Indian wind instruments and drums. Like many other religious celebrations throughout Chile, the festival at Andacolla began among the

A rodeo, Chile's alternative to bull-fighting. The aim is to force the steer against the stockade so that it is unable to move. It is then released, unharmed

Indians before the Spanish settlers brought Christianity to the country. Then, when so many Indians became Christian, the Church allowed them to fit their old Indian religious customs into Christian beliefs and traditions.

Some of La Serena's visitors come from Argentina, by a direct road across the Andes. However, most road traffic across the Andes takes a route further south, through the La Cumbre Pass near Mount Aconcagua. The Argentinians, who own the eastern half of this pass, call it the Uspallata. Halfway through it, on a slope of red rock, stands the famous statue Cristo Reden-

82

tor (Christ the Redeemer), more often called the Christ of the Andes. This marks the border between Chile and Argentina. An international railway also runs through La Cumbre/Uspallata but this has recently stopped carrying passengers.

Passengers within Chile may travel on the line as far as some of the country's most popular centres for ski-ing and other snow sports—including Portillo, where world ski-ing championships have taken place, and where a world ski-speed record has been established. There are snow sports areas too in the southern half of Chile; for example, to the east of Chillán, where there is also hot-spring bathing; and on Mount Llaima, near Temuco in Forest Chile. Mount Llaima is a beautifully-shaped volcano, and an active one. Its smoking crater is about 3,050 metres (10,000 feet) high, but the snow sports take place about halfway up. Even there, the sulphury smell of drifting volcano smoke is sometimes very strong.

The Chillán snow slopes are also on a volcano, but this is a dormant one although there is no saying when it might wake up. There is certainly some underground activity in the area, as is shown by the fact that the city of Chillán has twice been almost wholly demolished by earthquakes.

Chillán is the centre of a prosperous farming and wine-making district. It lies inland from the steel-making city of Concepción. It has about 120,000 people, makes leather goods, including the highly decorated equipment worn and used by *huasos,* and is famous as the birthplace of President Bernardo

O'Higgins. Captain Arturo Prat, the heroic Chilean leader in the naval battle at Iquique, was also a local man, but he was born in the Chillán district, not in Chillán itself.

Though still in the central zone, Chillán is about 400 kilometres (250 miles) south of Santiago. Temuco is further south by another 240 kilometres (150 miles). That puts it almost in the middle of Forest Chile, on the northern edge of the Lake District.

This is Indian territory. Most of the remaining full-blooded Mapuche Indians live in or fairly close to Temuco; and many of the city's 160,000 other inhabitants have a large proportion

A Mapuche Indian woman weaving outside her home near Temuco—note the traditional design of the house

of Mapuche blood. Traditional Mapuche clothing is often seen in the city. Mapuche cloth, jewellery, pottery and other hand-craft products are on sale everywhere. But a visitor has to go about 30 kilometres (19 miles) out of the city before he sees any of the old-style Indian houses, which are circular in shape, and made wholly of thatching straw.

In Temuco itself, the buildings of the city centre are very modern. There are even one or two skyscrapers. As for houses, they—like houses everywhere in Forest Chile—are nearly all made of wood. Even the roofs are covered with wooden shingles instead of tiles, and—because this is the wet end of the country—the roofs are also usually steeply pitched, to be quickly rid of rain and thawing snow.

East of Temuco, around the foot of smoking Mount Llaima, are two of Chile's fifty national parks. One of these is called *Los Paraguas,* the Umbrellas, because many of its trees look a little like umbrellas. These trees are native to Chile, and are called Chile pines. (In English-speaking countries they are often better known as monkey puzzles.)

Although native to Chile, Chile pines do not grow well all over the country. Nor do most other native trees. In the last century, however, it was found that the Australian gum-tree (the eucalyptus) would grow very happily in places where other trees would not thrive. Now there are so many gum-trees in Chile that they seem almost as native as the monkey puzzle.

Apart from Temuco, Forest Chile has three towns big enough to be called cities. These are Valdivia, Osorno and Puerto

Montt. All south of Temuco and in the Lake District, they are strung out from north to south about 100 kilometres (62 miles) apart, and have one feature in common. In appearance and atmosphere, they are more like towns in southern Germany or in parts of Switzerland than in Spain or an ex-Spanish colony. And the farming districts around them, as well as many of the smaller towns and the people, seem to match.

The reason becomes clear to the visitor when he meets some of the people, or hears their names, or finds that it is just as easy to buy a locally-made German sausage as it is to buy some such Chilean snack as the pasty of meat, onions, olives, raisins and hard-boiled egg called an *empanada*. He can buy German sausage and almost imagine that he is in southern Germany because this part of Chile began to attract German settlers a little over a hundred years ago. They were never in a majority, and they became loyal Chileans, but they have managed to impose a good deal of the German way of life on their corner of the ''New World''.

The middle city of the three, Osorno, is at the Chilean end of two other routes between Chile and Argentina. Travellers may make the whole journey by road, first along the shore of a very large lake with bird-thronged islands; and then across a lake-studded forest against a background of volcanoes. Or they may ''lake-hop'', going by ferry-boat through some of the most beautiful lakes, and travelling by road between the lakes and at either end of the journey. This route, too, is in sight of volcanoes and other Andean peaks.

Mount and Lake Osorno, in southern Chile

The road running south from Osorno also skirts lakes and leads to a ferry-boat. This one goes from the city of Puerto Montt across a sea-channel to the large island of Chiloé—the most northerly island of Archipelagic Chile. Chiloé was the last part of Chile to be held by Spanish royalists against the Chileans who were fighting for independence. Rather than surrender to the republicans, these royalists asked Britain to take over the island and make it part of the British Empire. But Britain had very good reasons for keeping on friendly terms with the new republic, and so said ''No, thank you''.

Chiloé's main farm crop is—as it has always been—potatoes. Much of the island is still heavily forested, and most of its 150,000 people live on or near the coast, so that they can fish as well as farm. They are also expert at traditional crafts, and hold an annual craft fair which attracts many visitors.

As in Chile's other forested areas, the houses—and the 150 churches—on Chiloé are nearly all made of wood. In some of the coastal areas, they are raised above the shore on tall wooden posts, so that high tides will not flood them.

South of Chiloé and the settled mainland opposite, there is no town for over one thousand cold, wet and windy kilometres (620 miles). Nor is there any road across that distance. Travellers to the far south must fly, or take a very fine five-day voyage in one of the passenger ships which ply regularly through the Archipelago, between Puerto Montt and Punta Arenas.

Punta Arenas, on the northern shore of the Magellan Strait, is a naval base, and the centre of southern Chile's important sheep-raising industry. The sheep farms, mainly begun by British settlers, are on both sides of the Magellan Strait, but the largest is on the south side, in Chilean Tierra del Fuego. It is said to have over one million sheep. Chile's part of Tierra del Fuego has a recently developed oil and natural gas town, Manantiales, as well as a much older settlement called Porvenir, where the people are mainly of Yugoslav descent.

Back on the mainland side of the Magellan Strait, there is an area to the north of Punta Arenas called Ultima Esperanza (Last Hope). Here, with a very impressive background much like the Norwegian fiords, is the town of Puerto Natales, which has become a base for tourists who can withstand the climate. However, the town does not make its living by tourism. Most of the men cross daily into Argentina, to work in the coal-mines, although Chile, too, has coal-mines in this area.

The great naturalist Charles Darwin studied wildlife on the coastlands of southern Chile, while a passenger on a British warship called *Beagle*. During the voyage, *Beagle's* officers charted a passage between Tierra del Fuego and some islands to the south, and called the passage Beagle Channel. Later, bad feeling arose between Chile and Argentina because Chile laid claim to some of the Beagle Channel islands, including one named Navarino.

The bad feeling still exists, especially as Chile now has a naval base on Navarino, as well as a small town called Puerto Williams, in honour of a British sailor named John Williams, who made the Magellan Strait a Chilean possession. Puerto

Wooden houses raised on posts, on Chiloé Island

Williams is a very small town, but a pleasant one. Apart from serving the naval base, it lives by canning crabs for export. Now it is beginning to attract occasional visitors because of its varied wildlife. Visitors also like to feel that they have come not only to the end of settled Chile, but also to the earth's most southerly town.

Following Robinson Crusoe

The castaway hero of Daniel Defoe's famous story *Robinson Crusoe* was an imaginary character. However, much of the story—including the goat—came to Defoe from a real castaway. He was Alexander Selkirk, a Scot who had spent several years marooned on an island of the Juan Fernandez group in the Pacific Ocean, about 640 kilometres (400 miles) due west of Valparaiso.

There are three islands in the group. They were discovered in 1574 by a Spaniard named Juan Fernandez, and they now belong to Chile. The smallest, only an islet, is called Santa Clara. The other two originally had the names Mas a Tierra (Nearer the Mainland) and Mas a Fuera (Further Away), but in 1966 the Chilean government decided to give them names that were more interesting, and more easily recognizable. So they are now called Robinson Crusoe and Alexander Selkirk. However, that is a little confusing to visitors, as the island on which Selkirk was marooned is not the island with his own name, but the larger of the two, Robinson Crusoe!

No doubt, life was lonely and anxious for Alexander Selkirk, but he at least had some comforts, as Robinson Crusoe could hardly be called a desert island. It has fertile soil, caves for shelter, a pleasant climate, flocks of wild goats, many trees and

The memorial to Alexander Selkirk on Robinson Crusoe Island

a plentiful supply of excellent sea food. In fact, the five hundred people who are now permanent residents there make a good living by exporting lobsters and other seafood to Chile, with which they have regular sea and air links.

Robinson Crusoe has an area of 93 square kilometres (36 square miles) but Chile has another Pacific island which is nearly twice as big. It is also about six times as far from Chile—3,700 kilometres (2,300 miles). This is Easter Island, or Isla de Pascua, as Spanish-speakers call it. It has the name Easter Island because the first Europeans to see it, the crew of a ship from Holland, arrived there on Easter Sunday 1722—fourteen years after Alexander Selkirk was rescued from what is now Robinson Crusoe Island.

92

Easter Island was once very well wooded, but early inhabitants cut down the trees and did not plant more, so most of it is now hilly grassland, although the grass is almost too thin for grazing in many places. The 1,500 inhabitants grow enough crops to feed themselves, and make money by exporting wool. Most of them are Pacific Islanders similar in descent to the Maoris of New Zealand and the Hawaiian people.

For visitors, the great attraction of Easter Island is about six hundred huge statues carved from the island's soft volcanic rock. These are 9 metres (30 feet) or more in height, weigh up to 8 tonnes (7.8 tons), have flattish faces and long ears, and are sometimes topped with tall-crowned hats. In the language of the islanders, they are called Moai, but the present islanders did not make them. Nobody knows who did, or why—although some people believe that the carvers were South American Indians from the old Inca kingdom.

Apart from some other islands—all very small—Chile has no other territory outside its own boundaries, but it claims a very large one—a piece of the Antarctic continent 1,250,000 square kilometres (485,000 square miles) in area. Chile cannot say that it actually owns this vast tract, as it has agreed to a United Nations treaty suspending all such claims. However, it has permanent bases in the territory, and is doing much exploration and scientific work there.

Whether or not the territory will at last become Chilean must remain to be seen. It depends upon future United Nations policy and decisions and, of course, on the attitude of future Chilean

Some of the Moai, the huge Easter Island statues carved from volcanic rock

governments. The present Chilean government seems to be firmly established, and has managed to settle many of the problems which faced it and the country in 1973. But there have been no elections since 1970, nor will there be any before 1988/9. Until then, no one can safely say what Chile's future policy about Antarctica—or about anything else—will be.

94

Index

industries 34, 66, 77, 78, 83 *see also*
    factories
Iquique 76–78, 84
Italians, Italy 19, 20

La Cumbre Pass 82, 83
lakes 14, 76, 87, 88
La Moneda 65, 66
languages 9, 10, 12
La Serena 80–82
Lautaro 23
Lima 21, 26, 27

MacKenna, Vicuña 60
Magellan, Ferdinand 17
Magellan Strait 17, 89
mestizos 19, 36, 47
minerals, mining 8, 18, 21, 24, 36,
    48, 53, 54, 56, 76–80, 89
Mistral, Gabriela 81
museums 59, 80
music 63, 71, 81

national parks 75, 76, 85
Navarino 89
nitrates 31, 34, 35, 37, 48, 53, 76, 78
North, John 48

oases 8, 29, 74, 79
O'Higgins, Bernardo 26, 32, 33, 60,
    69, 83, 84
Osorno 85, 87

Pacific Ocean 14, 17, 20, 22, 35, 57,
    58, 91
Panama, Isthmus of 20
Peru, Peruvians 14, 21, 24–29, 32,
    34–36, 69, 73, 74, 77
Pinochet, General A. 40, 41
population 12, 16, 17, 19, 36, 38, 45,
    57, 67, 70, 72, 76, 78, 80, 83,
    84, 88, 93
Portales, Diego 33
Portillo 83
Portugal, Portuguese 7, 17
Porvenir 89
Prat, Captain A. 77, 83, 84
Puerto Montt 85, 86, 88

Puerto Natales 89
Puerto Williams 89, 90
Punta Arenas 88, 89

Quinta Vergara 70, 71

religion 29, 30, 38, 39, 58, 59, 81–83
rivers 8, 9, 22, 52, 60, 61, 63, 79
roads 56, 73, 76, 82, 87, 88
Robinson Crusoe Is. 91, 92
rodeos 52, 81

San Cristobal Hill 63
San Martin, Gen. José de 25, 27, 32
Santa Cruz, Andres de 33
Santa Lucia Hill 59, 60, 63
Santiago 22, 43, 44, 56, 59–67, 72,
    73, 80
Selkirk, Alexander 91, 92
Spain, Spanish 9, 19, 21–27, 29
    31–35, 48, 59, 69, 80, 86, 92
sports 62, 63, 72, 83

Temuco 84, 85
Tierra del Fuego 16–18, 89
tourism, tourists 56, 72, 75, 78, 81, 89
transport 33, 48, 55–57, 60, 68, 69,
    78, 83, 87, 88
Tucapel, Battle of 23

Ultima Esperanza 89
United Nations Organisation 93
U.S.A. 13, 44, 78
Uspallata Pass 82, 83

Valdivia, city of 22, 27, 59, 85
Valdivia, Pedro de 22, 23, 59
Valparaiso 56, 57, 66–69, 91
Videla, Gabriel G. 80
Viña del Mar 57, 67, 69–72
volcanoes 17, 76, 79, 80, 83, 85, 87

wars 23–28, 33, 35–37, 39, 72, 73,
    77, 78, 83
wildlife 13, 17, 64, 76, 87, 90, 91
Williams, John 89, 90

Yugoslavia, Yugoslavs 19, 34, 89

96